Pentatonics P

The 330 Pentatonic Scales for

Paperback Version

Fellow Guitarist,

This is the paperback version of the 330 pentatonic scales from www.pentatonics.pro. Thank you for purchasing this book, we are eternally grateful as this helps us to keep the site up and running. May your investment return to you tenfold and the time you spend with this material make you an outstanding improviser.

How to Use this Material

Please use this book in conjunction with the material on the website, here are the relevant links for you to get started:

Introduction
The Foundation
Practicing

In the remainder of this book, you'll find the starting pattern for each of the 330 pentatonic scales possible from permutating all available intervals into sets of five notes with the same root. It's not necessary to learn all these scale shapes as **the practice of finding groups of intervals and playing combinations you probably haven't explored before will do wonders for your improvisation skills**. I think you'll find it liberating for your fingers as well as your mind.

Remember, you can always take a scale you like the sound of and explore it further by mapping out the five patterns, and don't dismiss the ones with 3 or 4 semi-tones in a row; use these to practice chromatic playing with a metronome or beat. All scale examples are in A with the intervals marked on the diagram so that you can easily transpose them to other root notes. I **wouldn't** suggest playing the scales in the order they're laid out here; instead, choose a random page and if you find one you like, spend some time with it, ask yourself if you can find a use for it, or a chord that it works with. Try coming up with riffs and licks, record yourself and listen back, and above all be creative.

To your best playing yet,

Graham Tippett

www.unlocktheguitar.net

www.pentatonics.pro

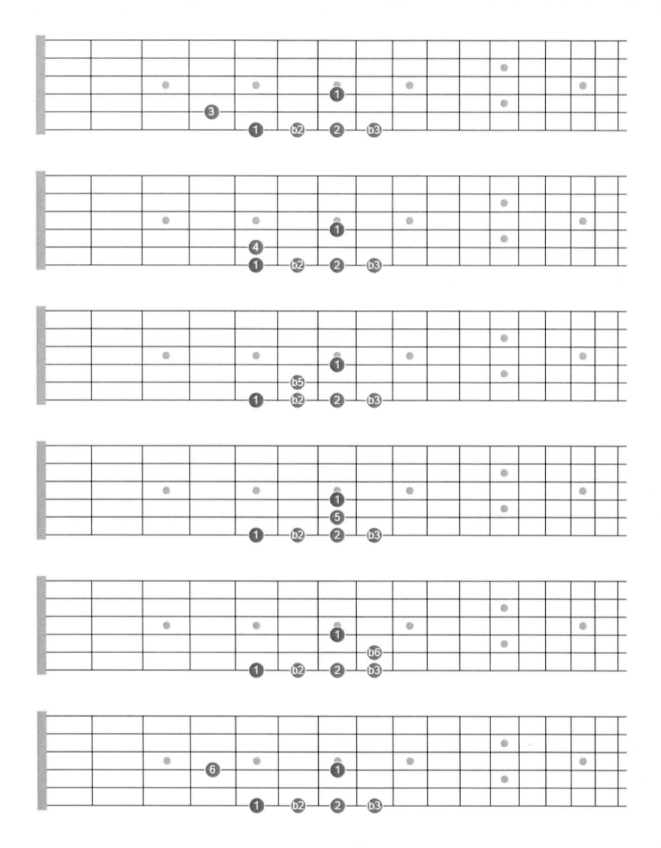

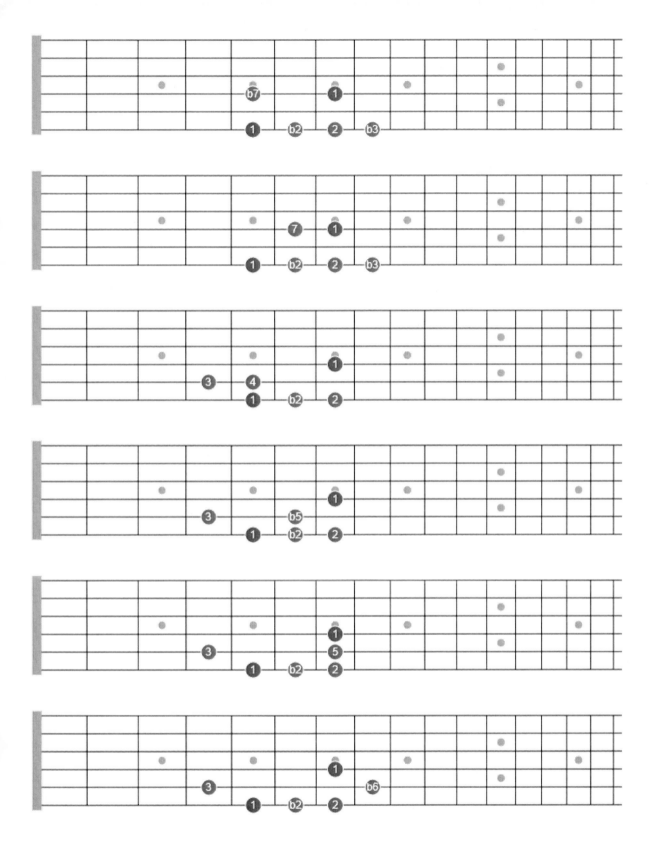

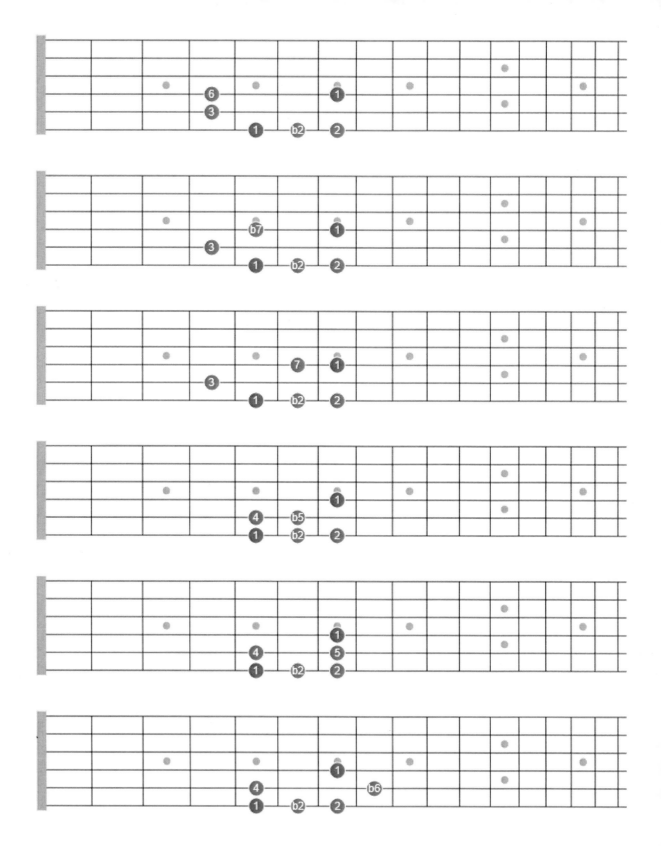

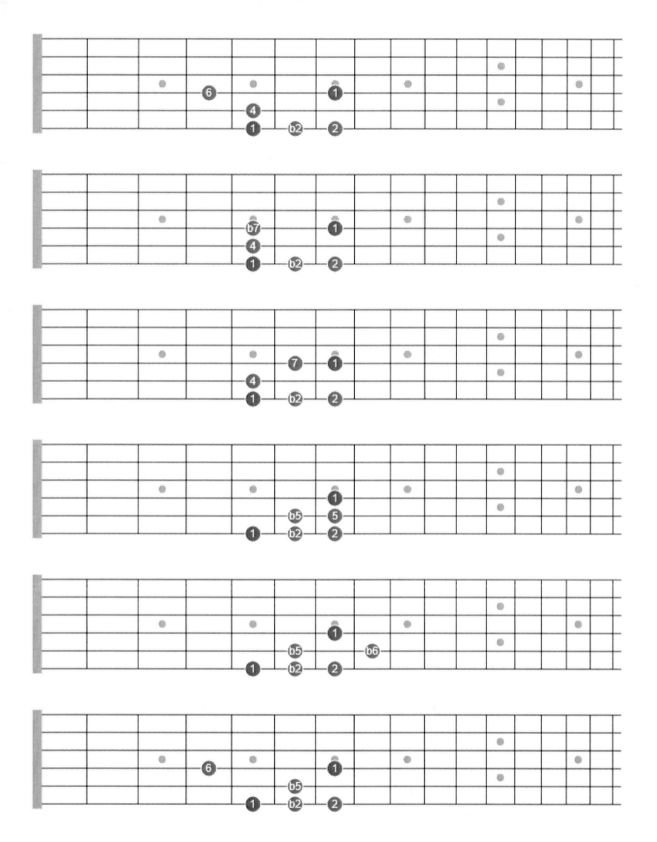

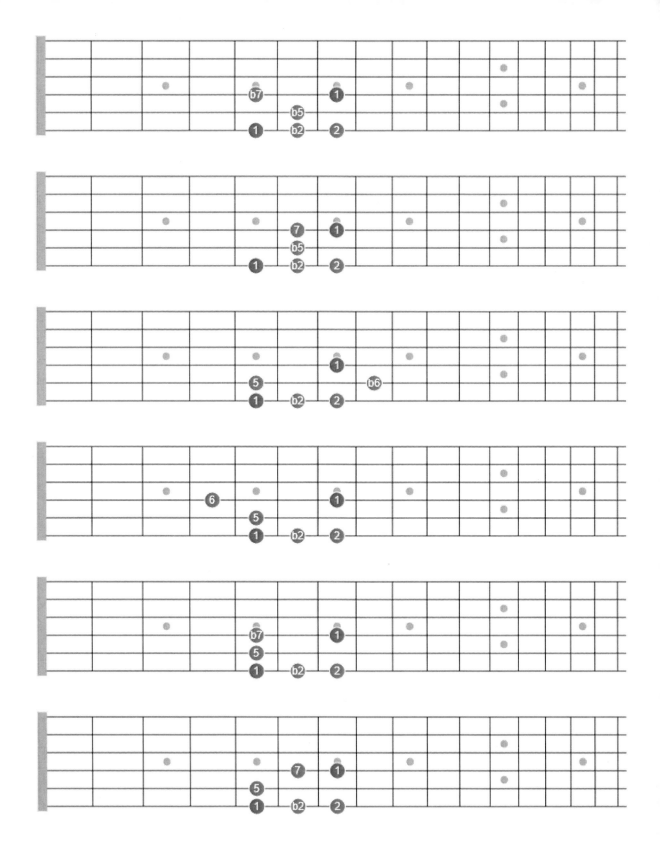

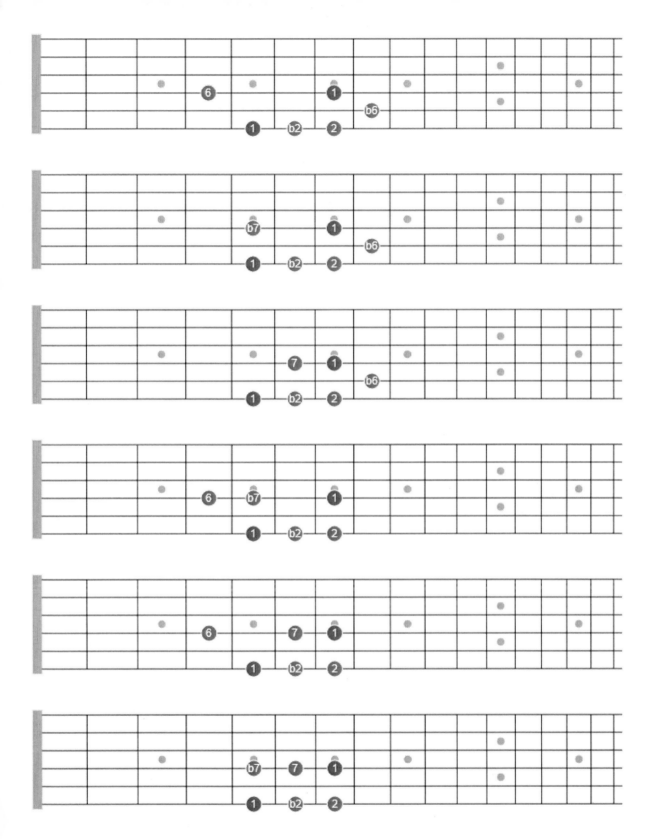

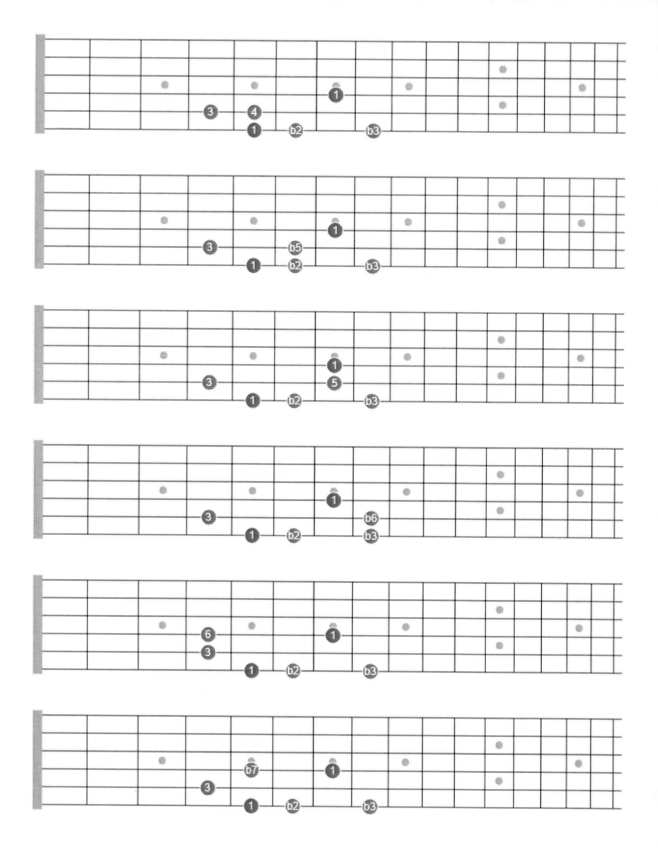

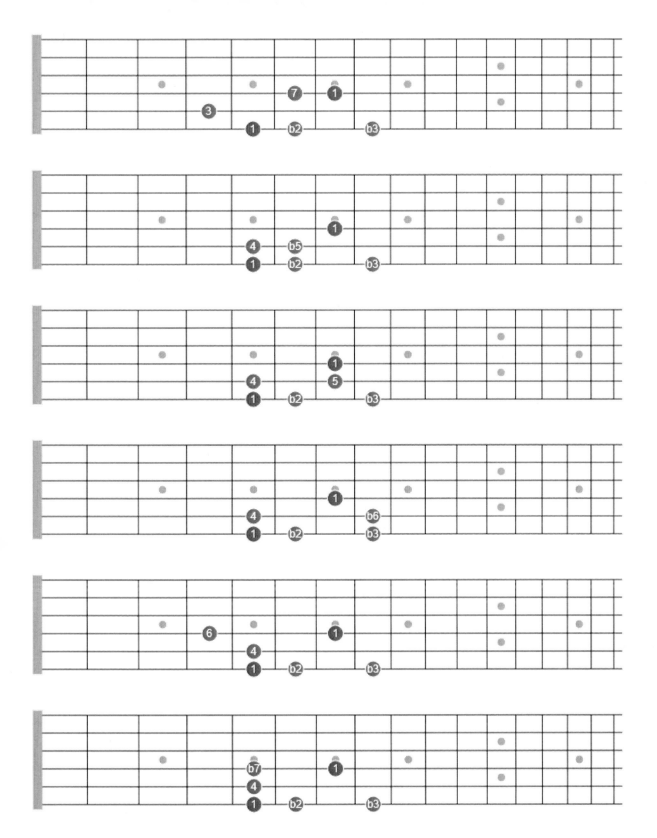

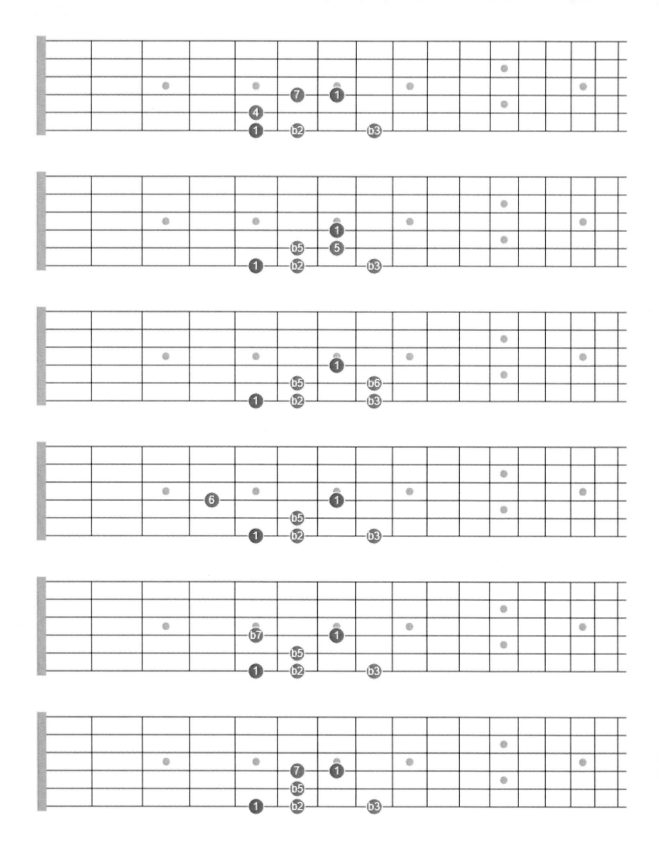

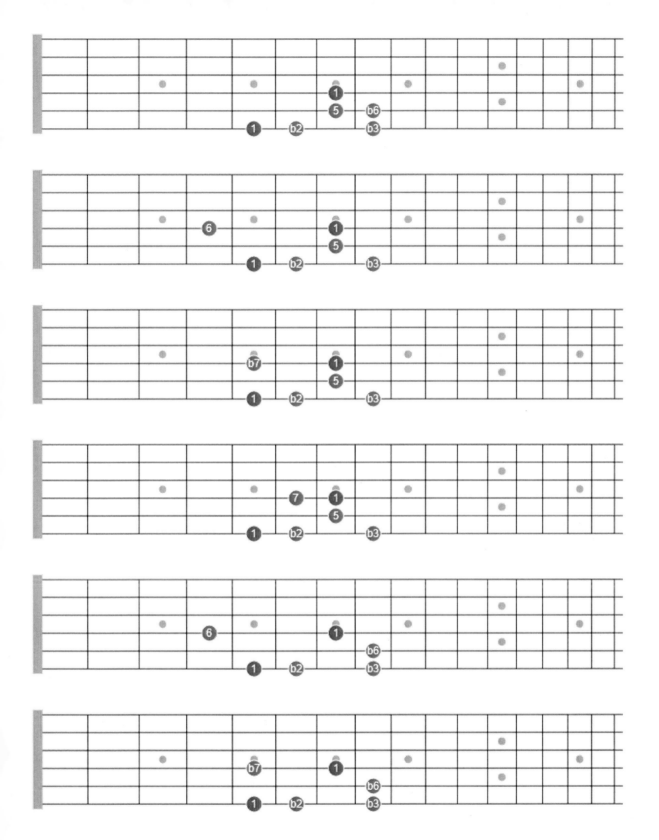

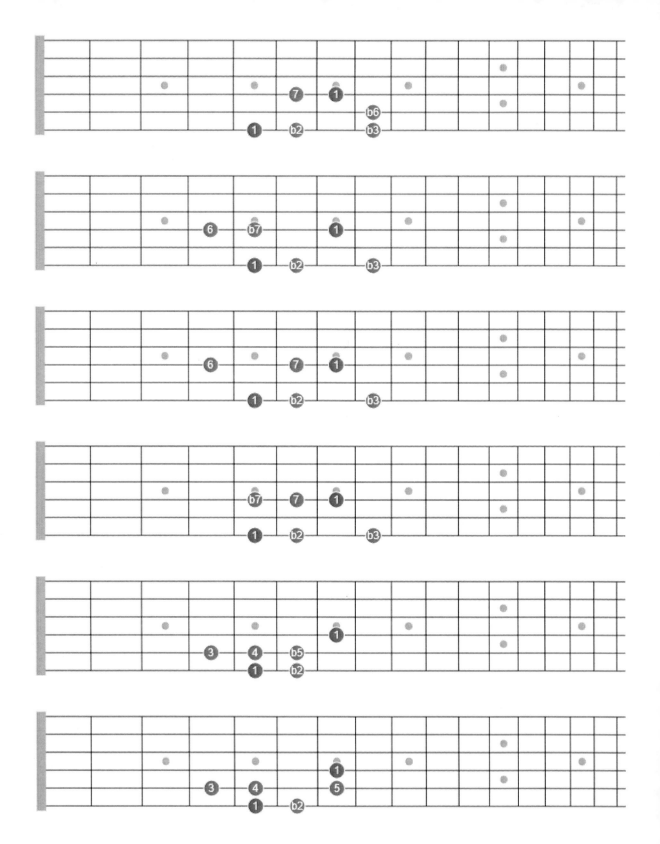

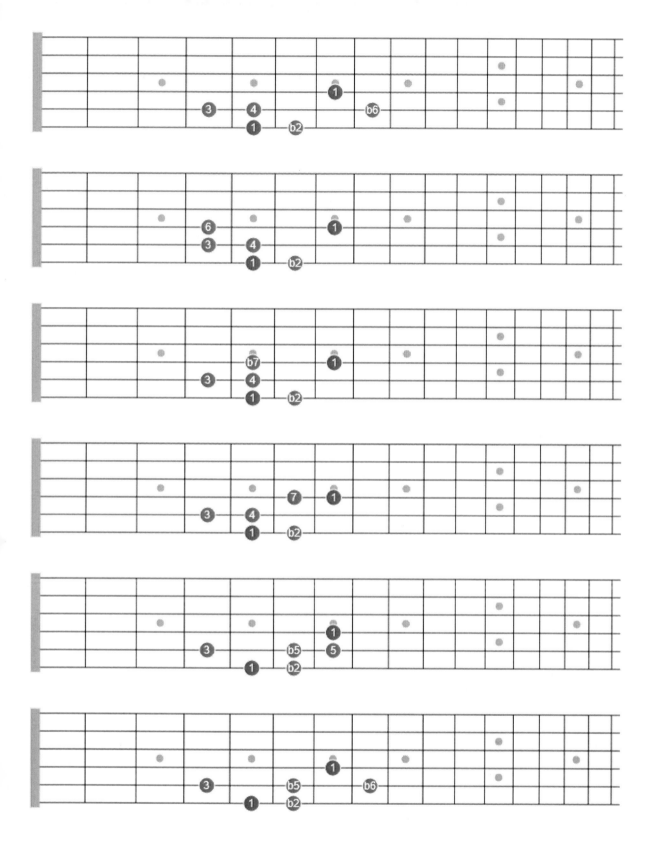

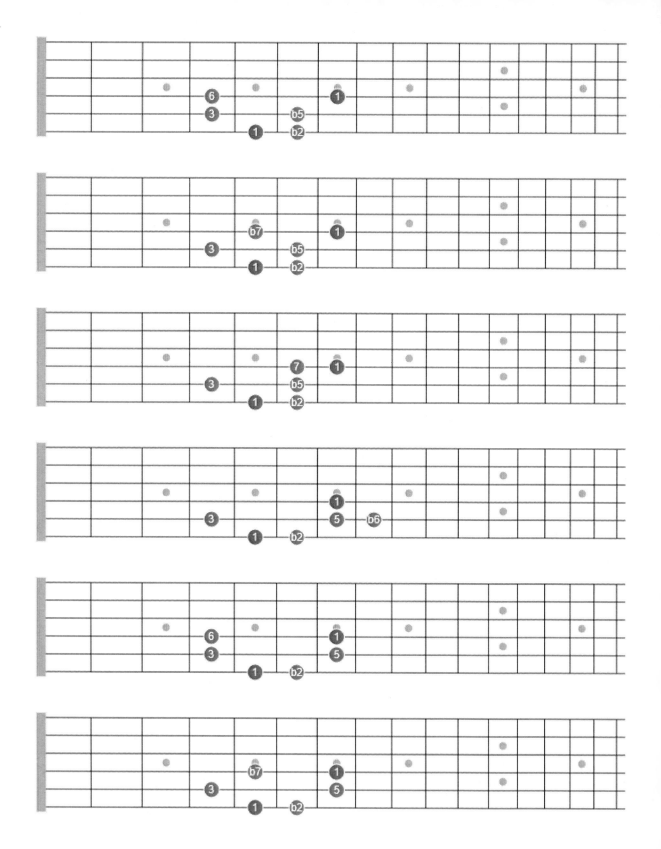

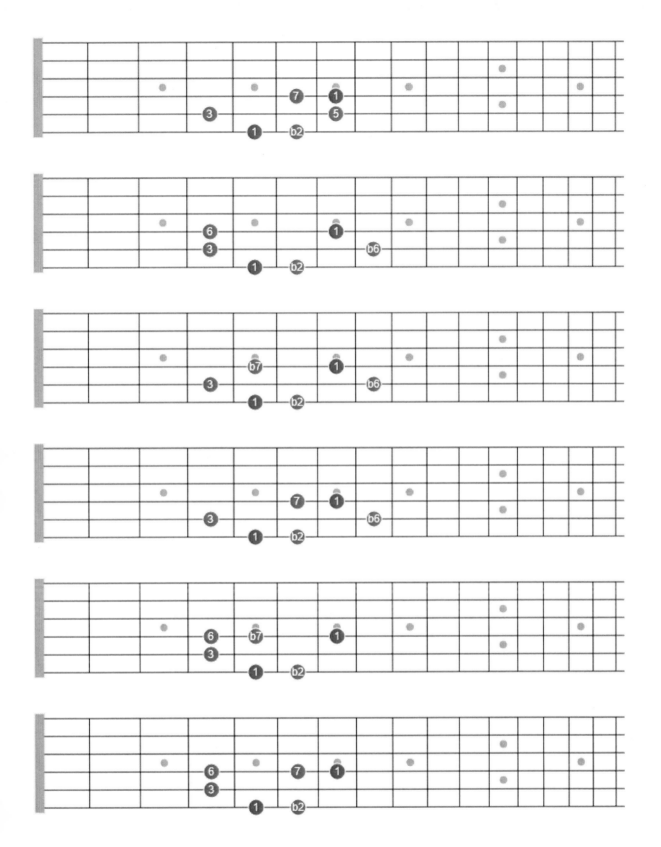

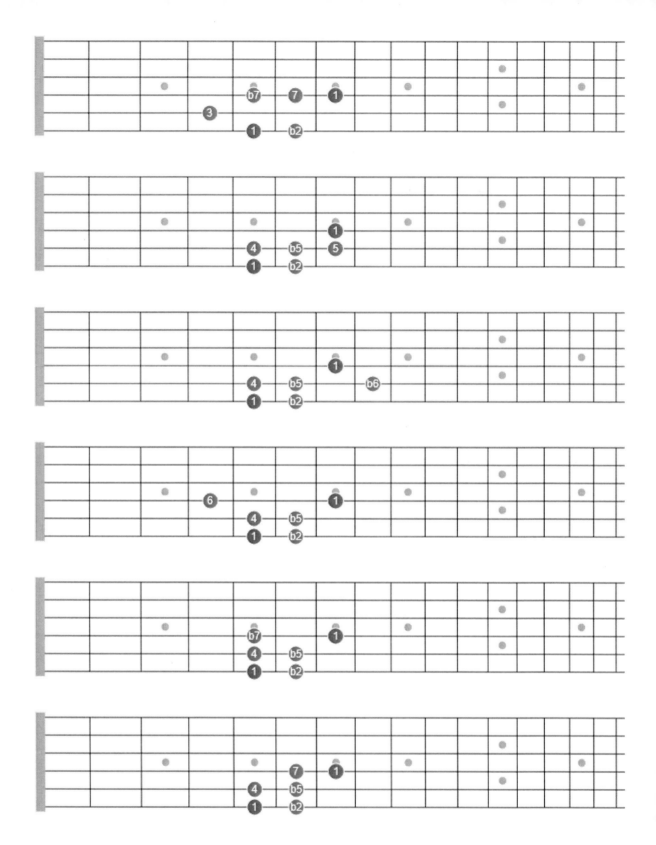

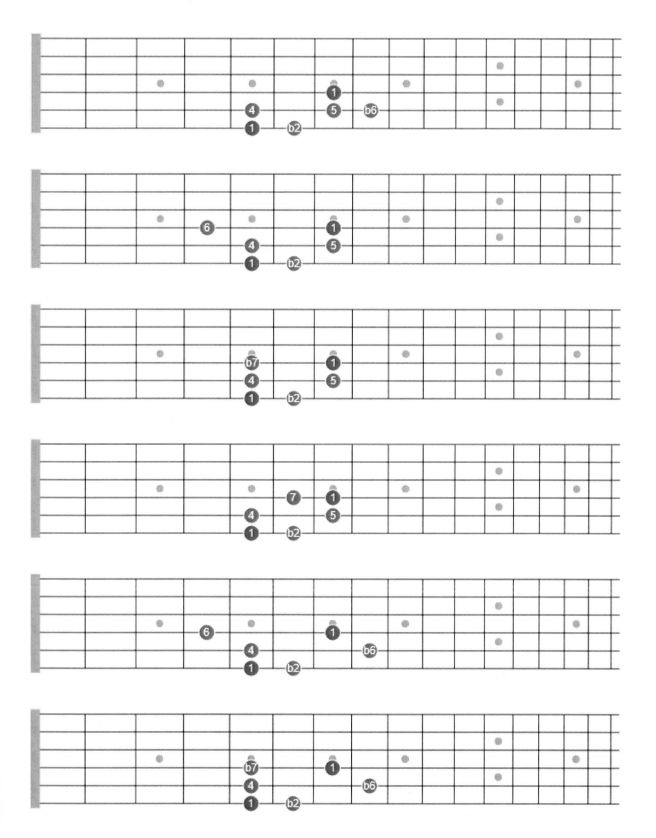

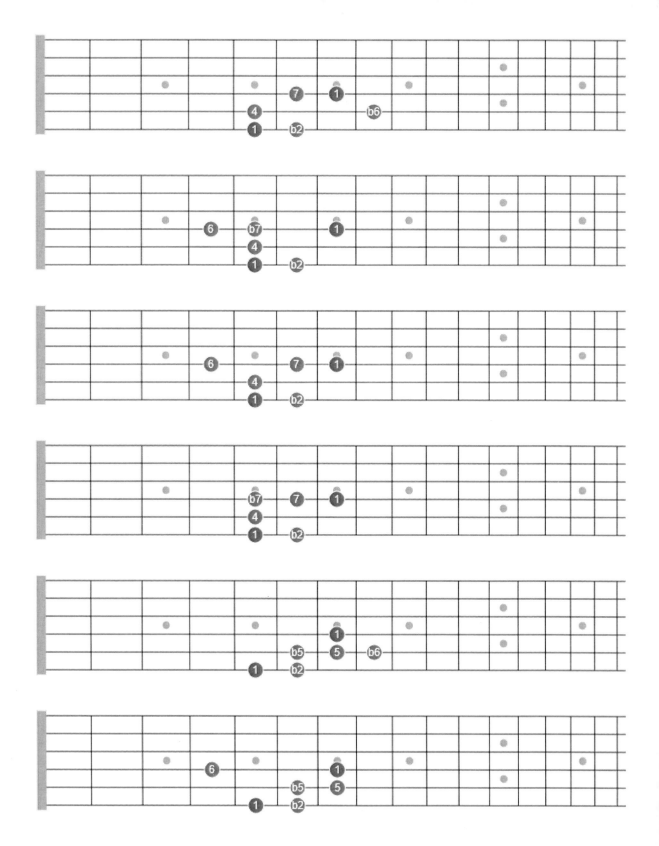

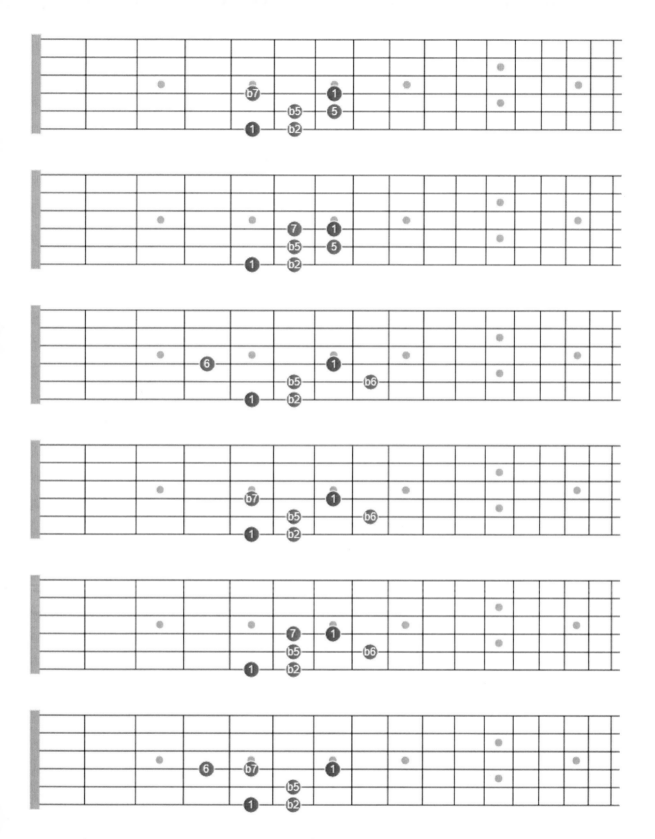

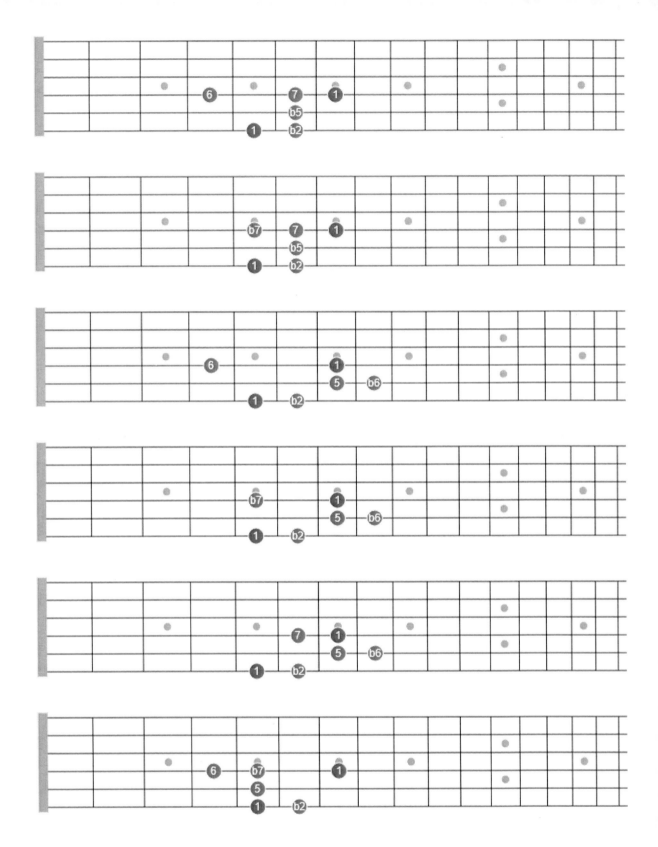

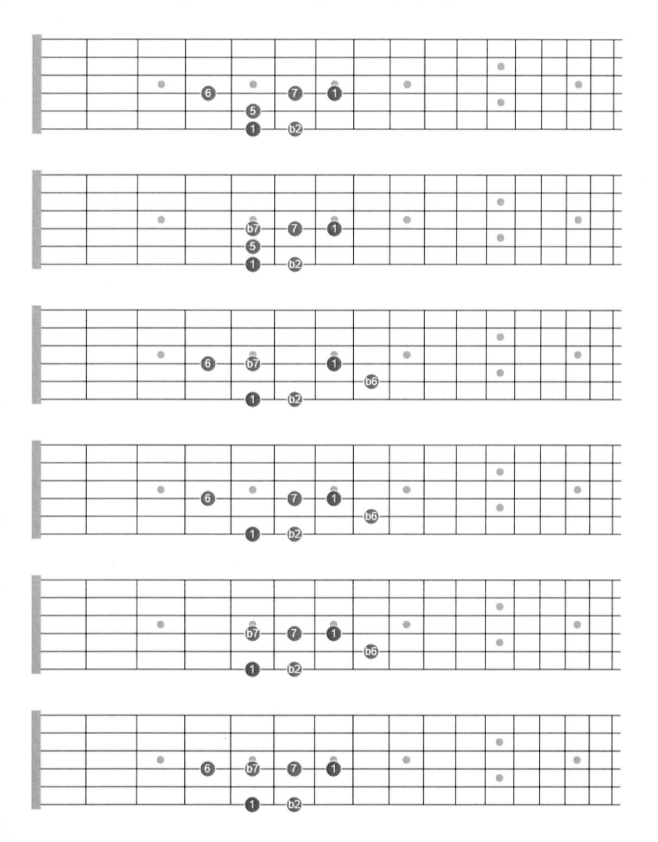

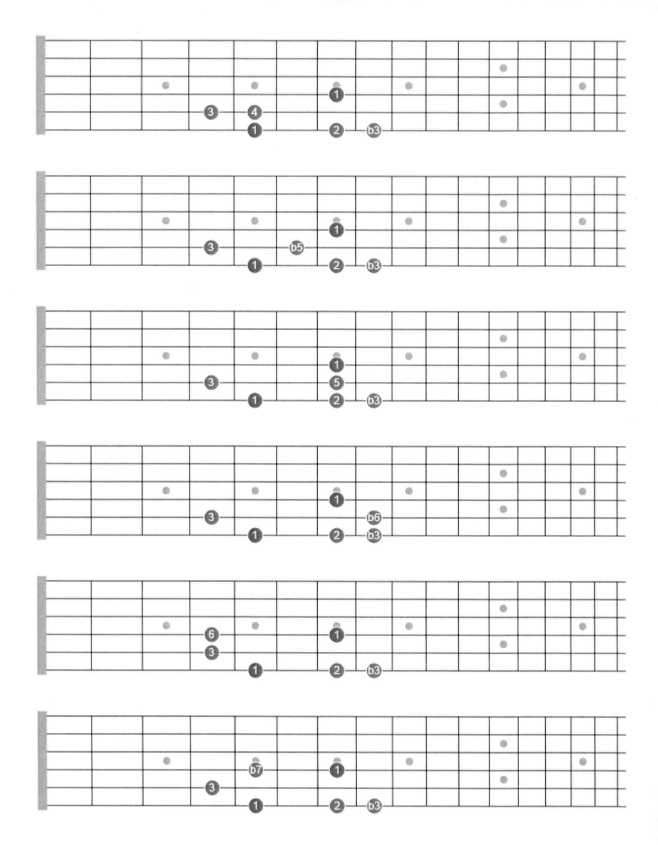

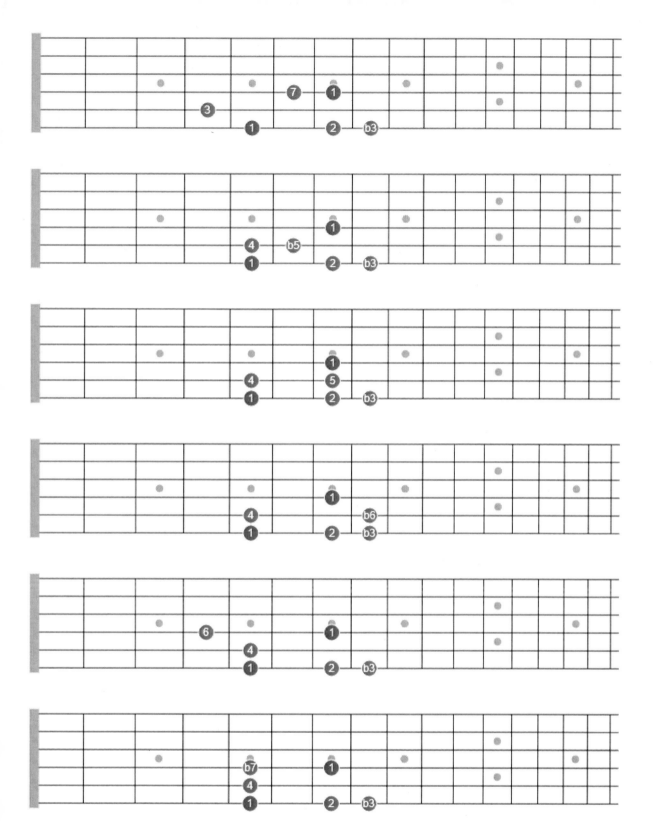

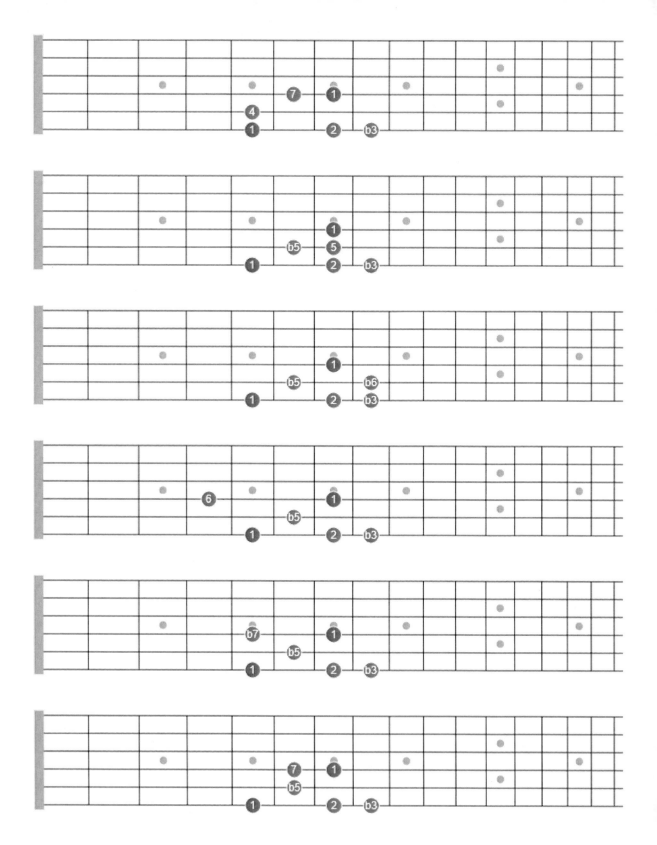

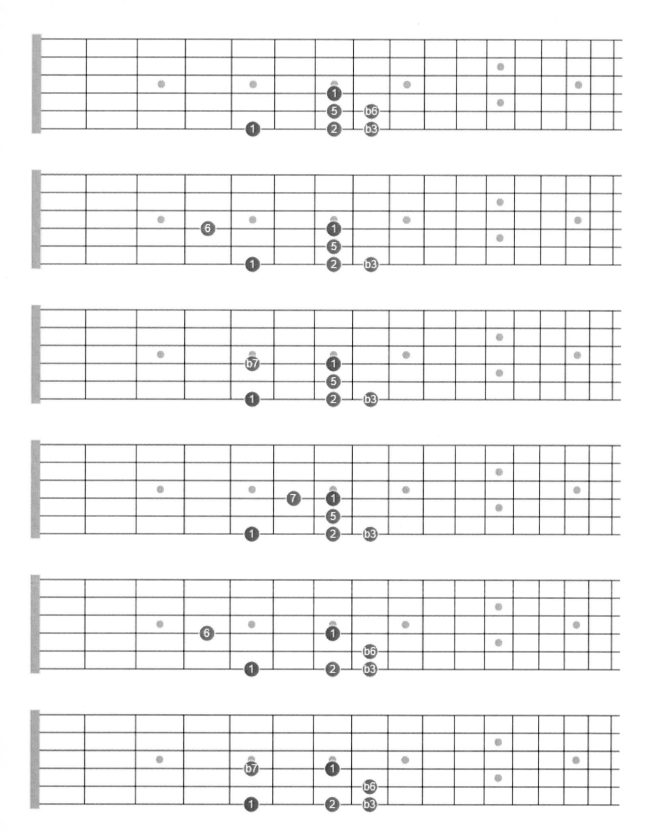

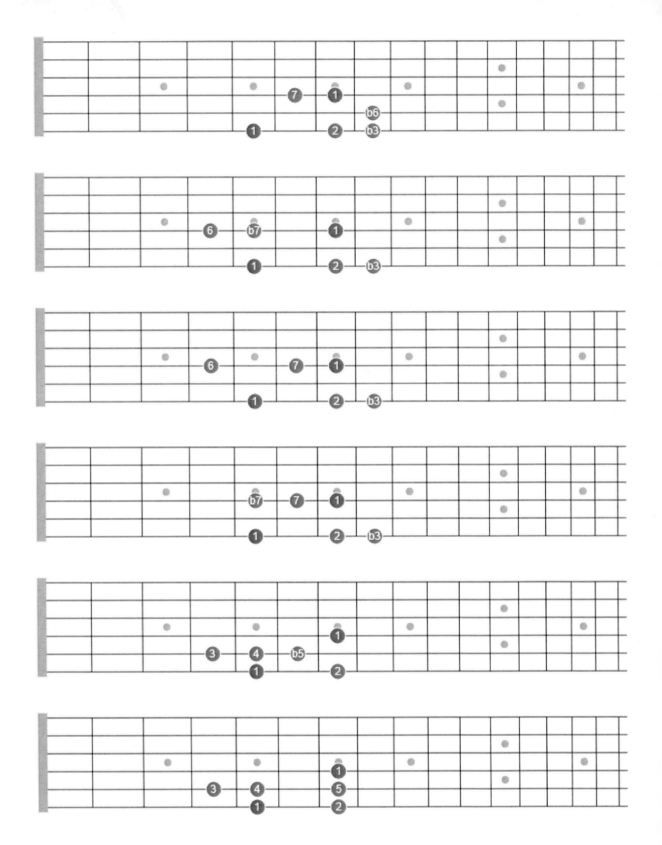

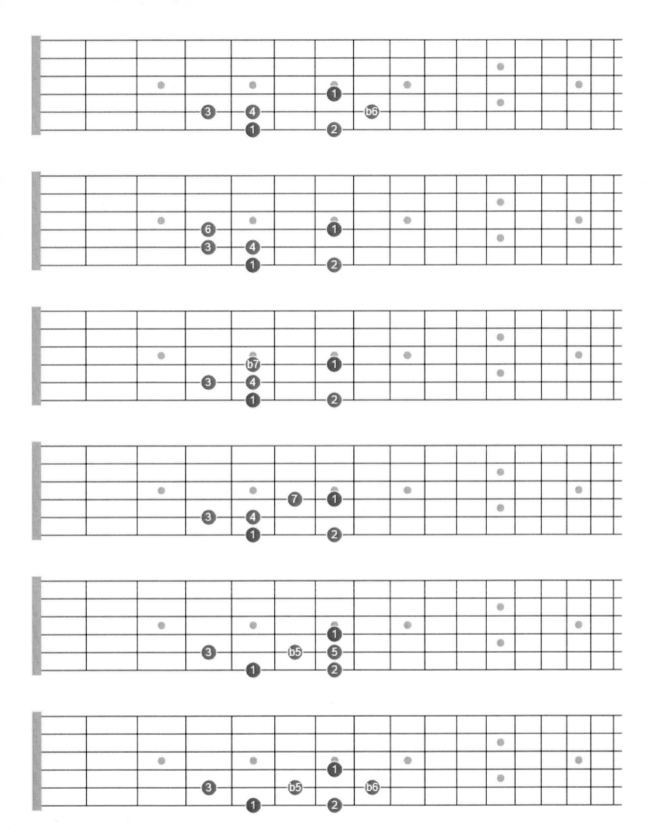

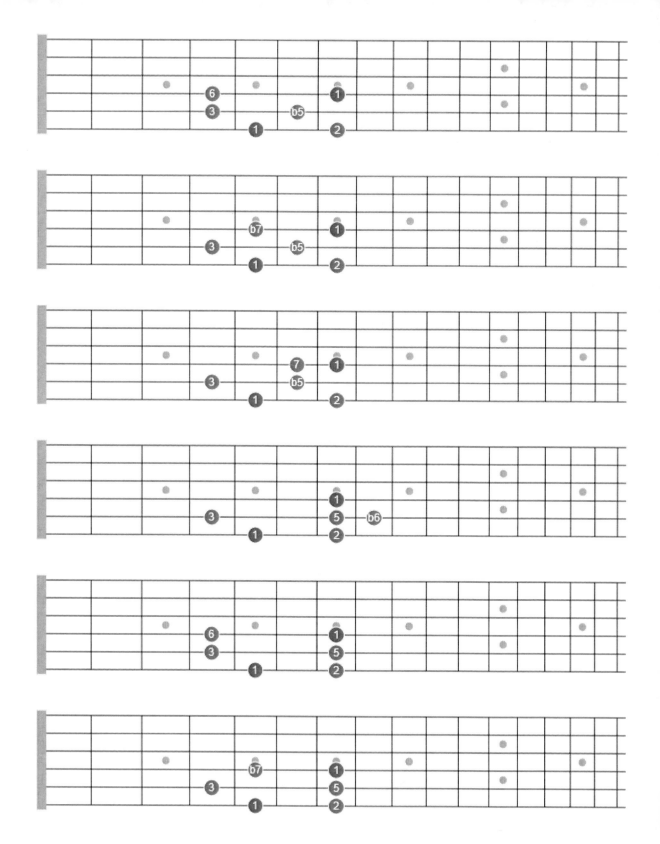

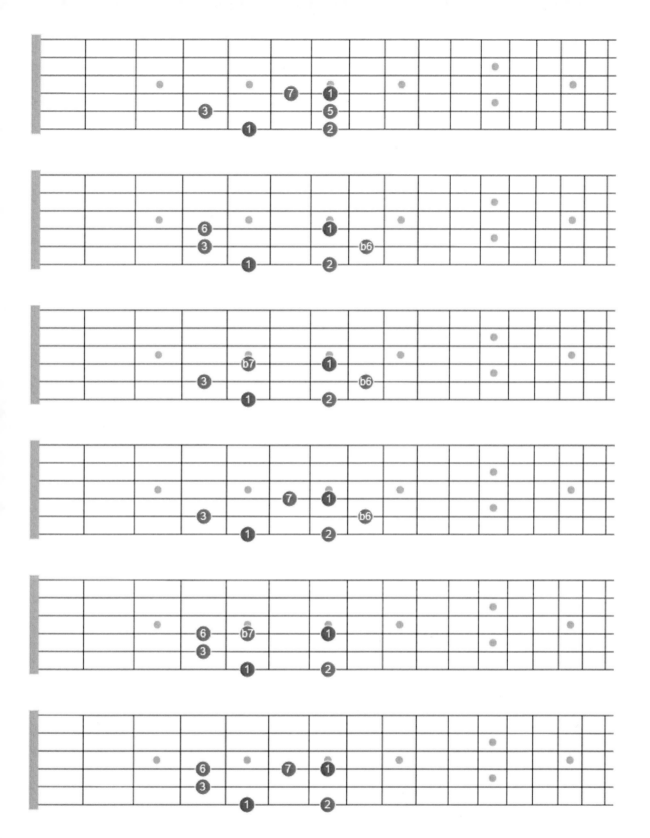

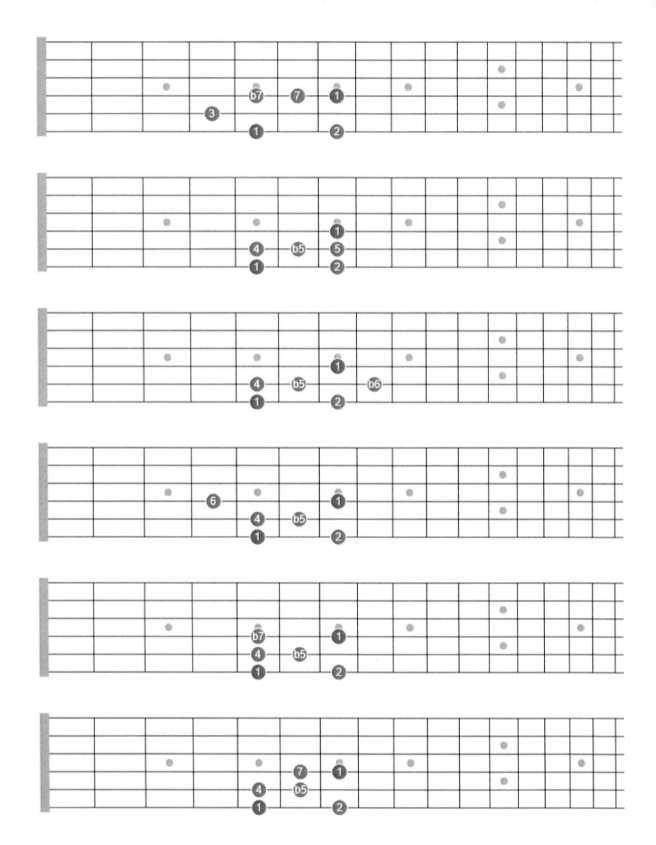

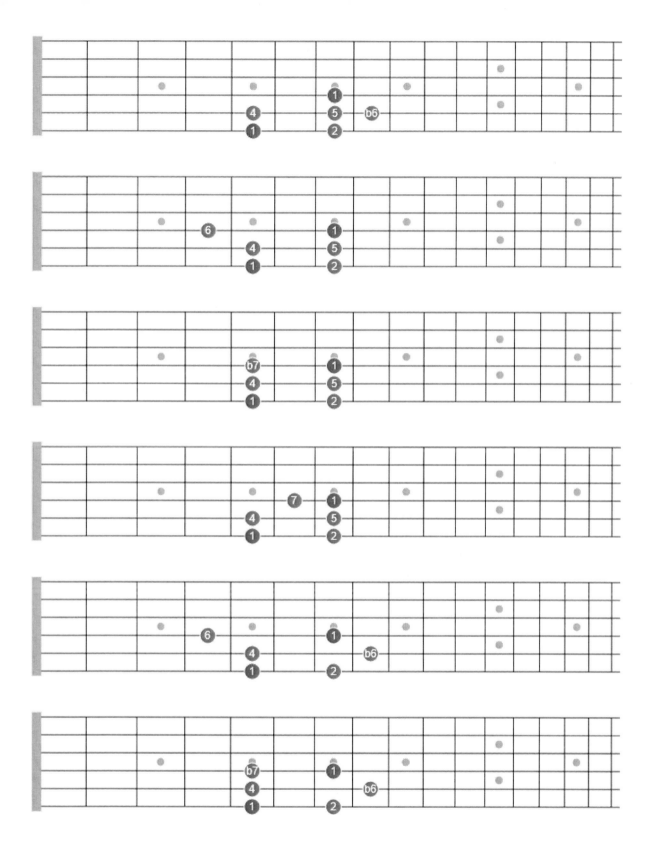

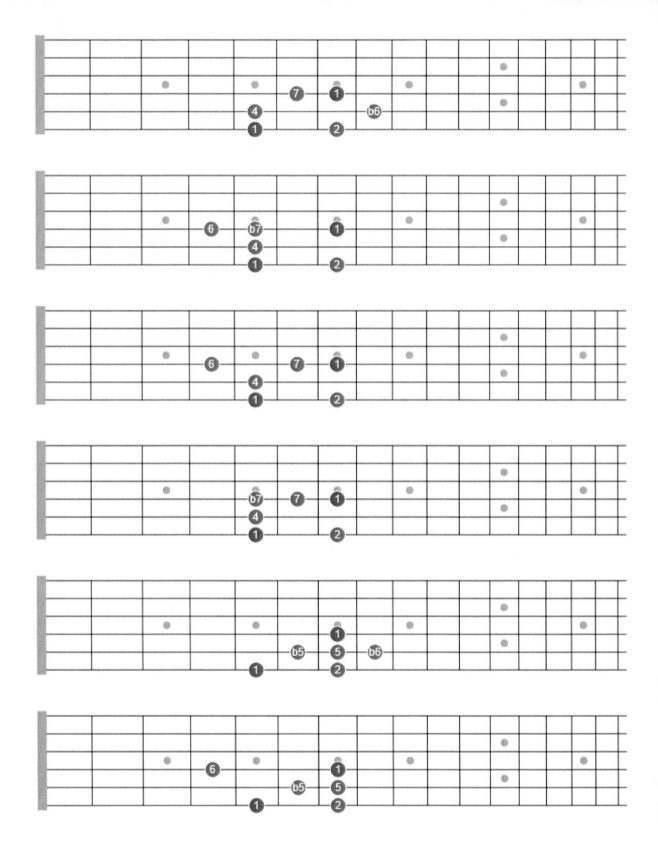

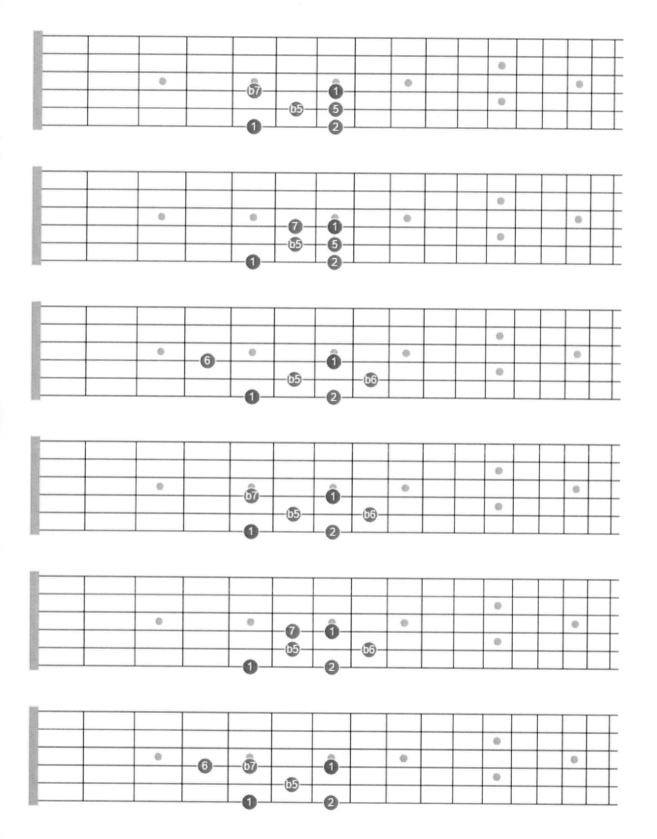

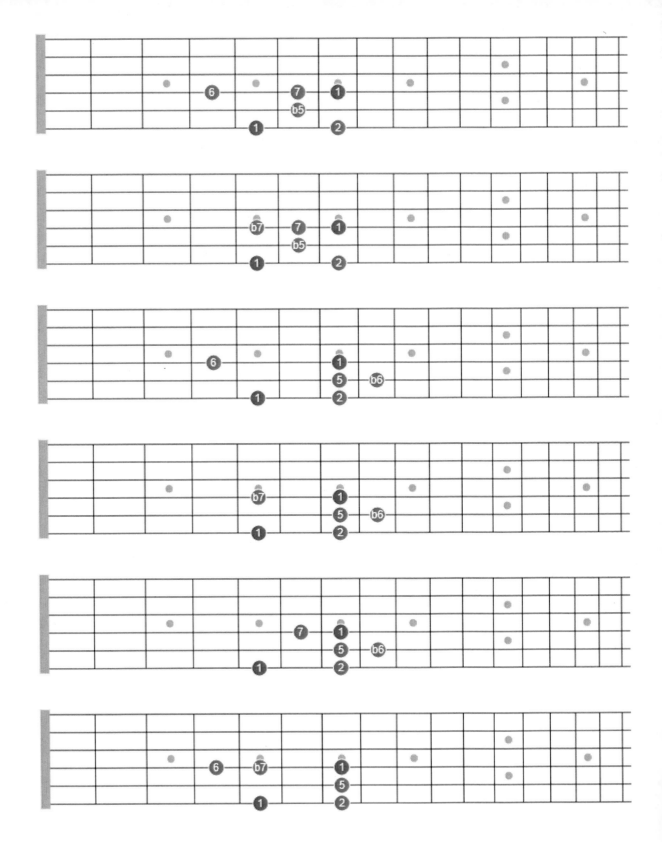

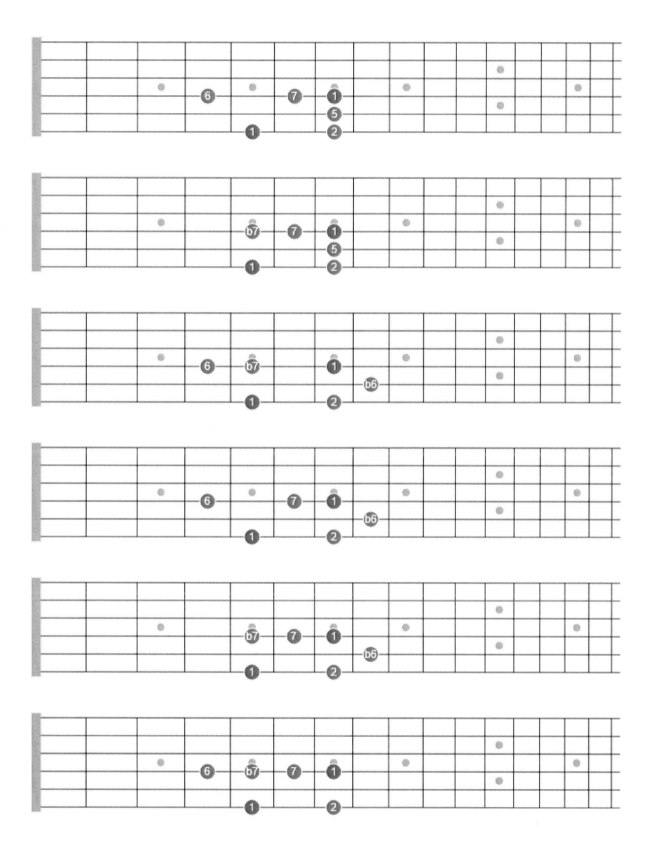

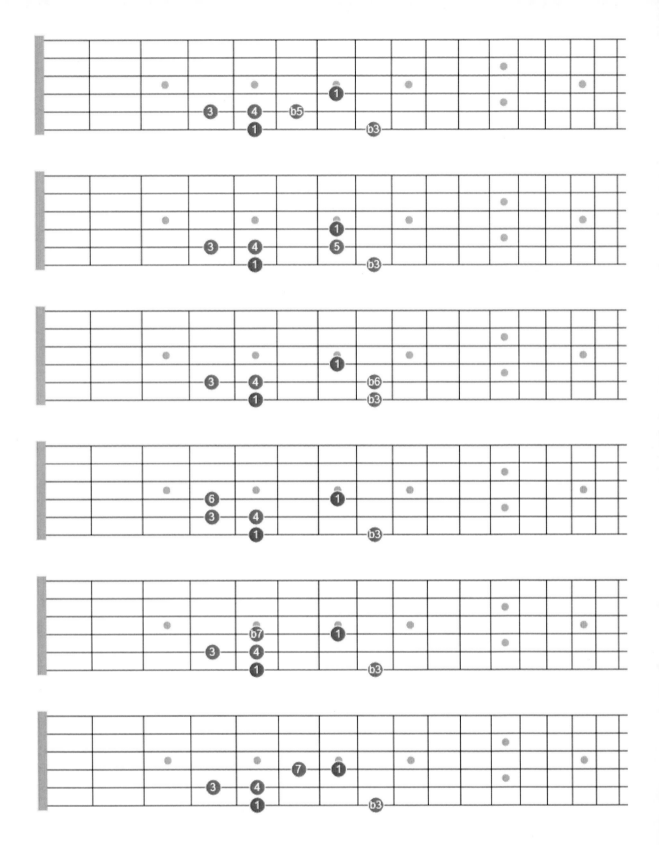

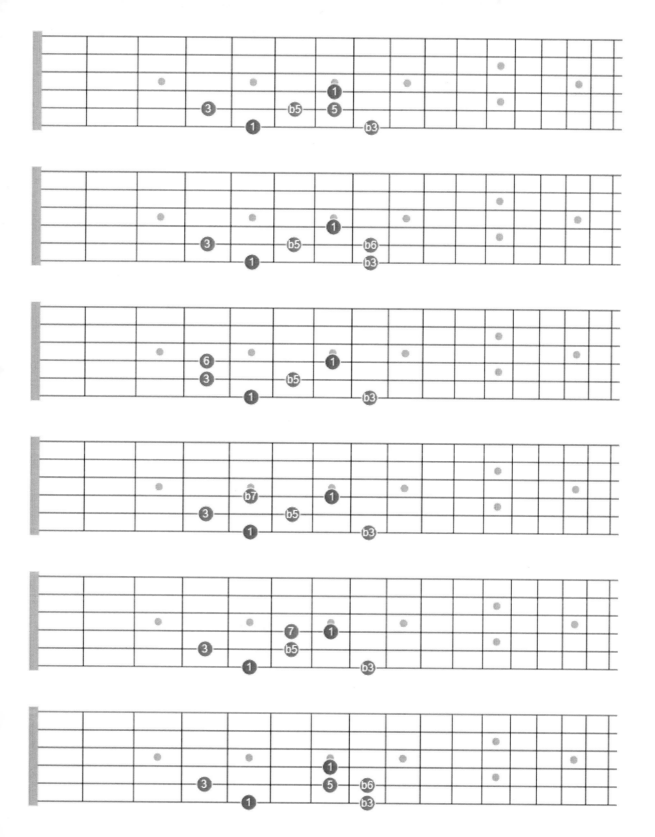

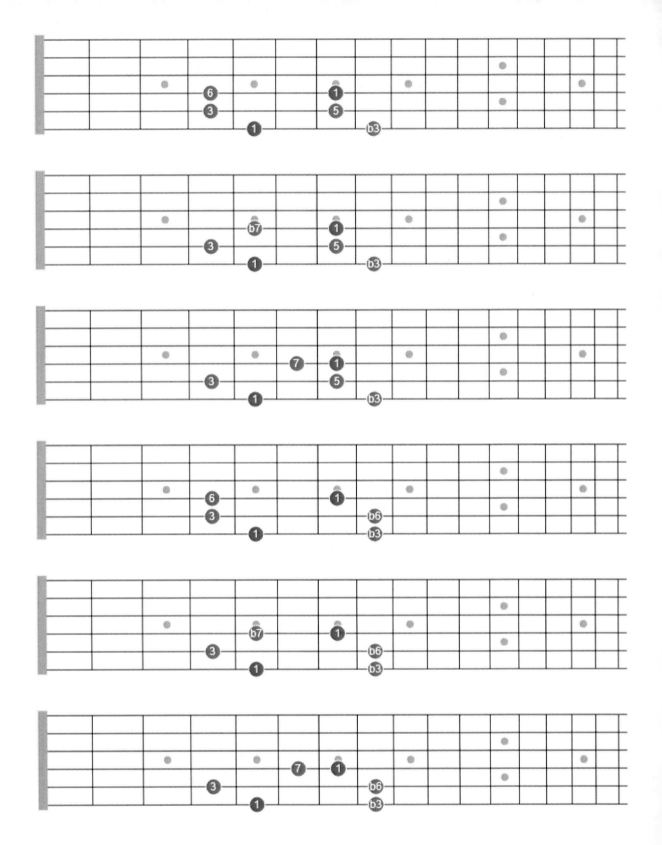

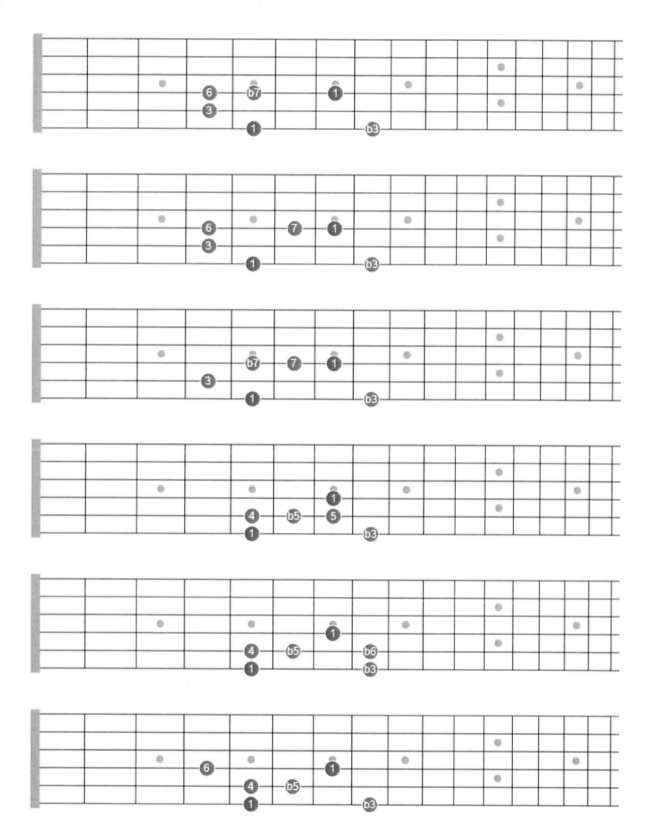

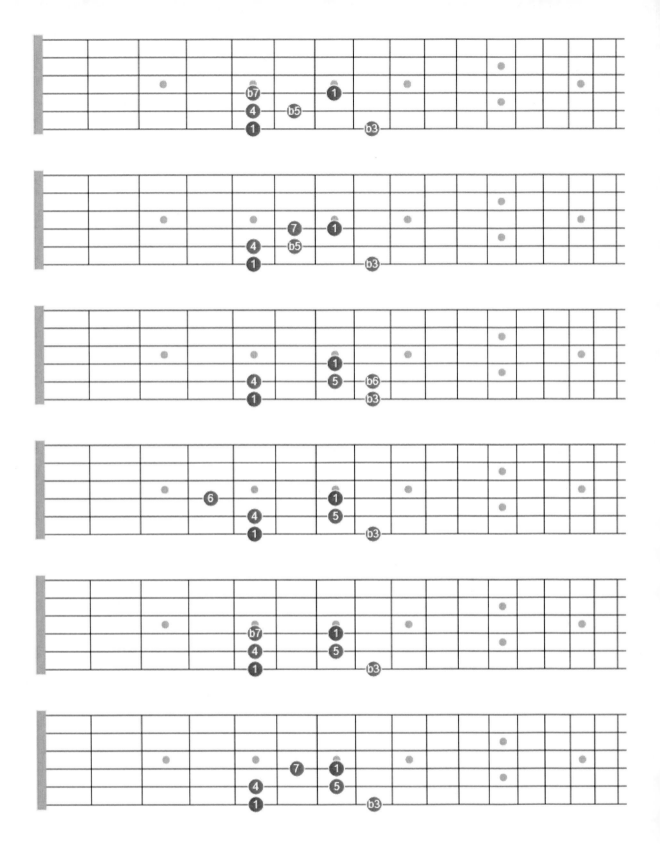

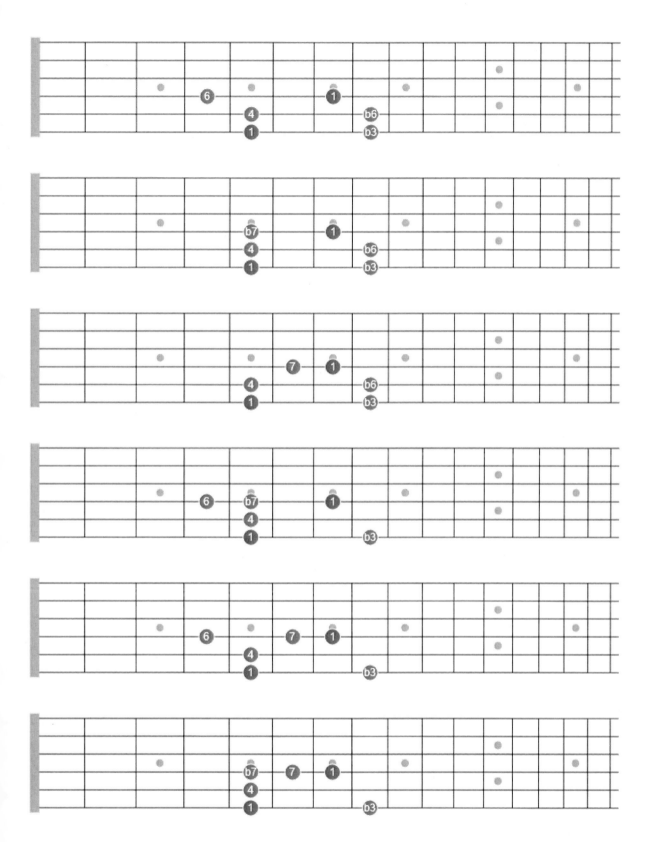

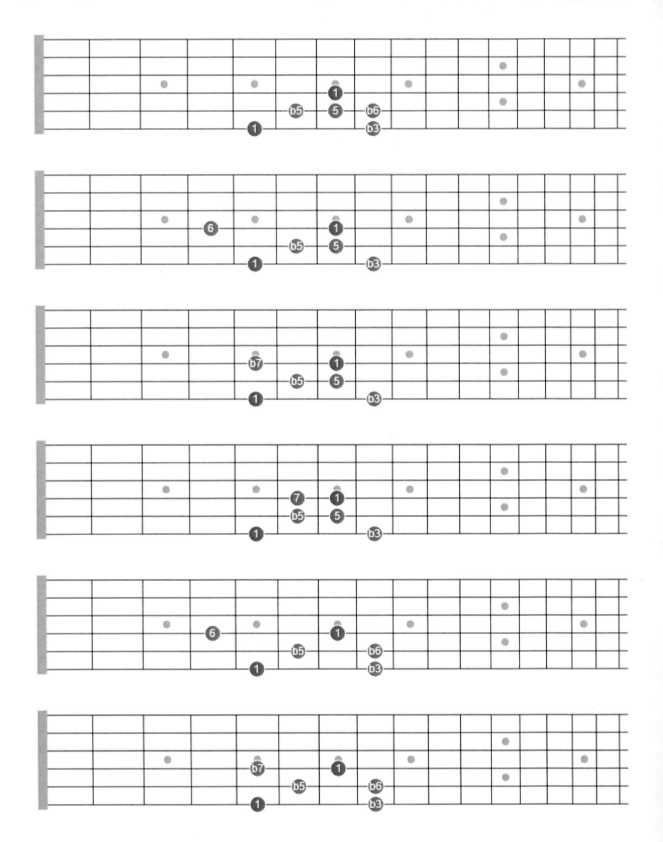

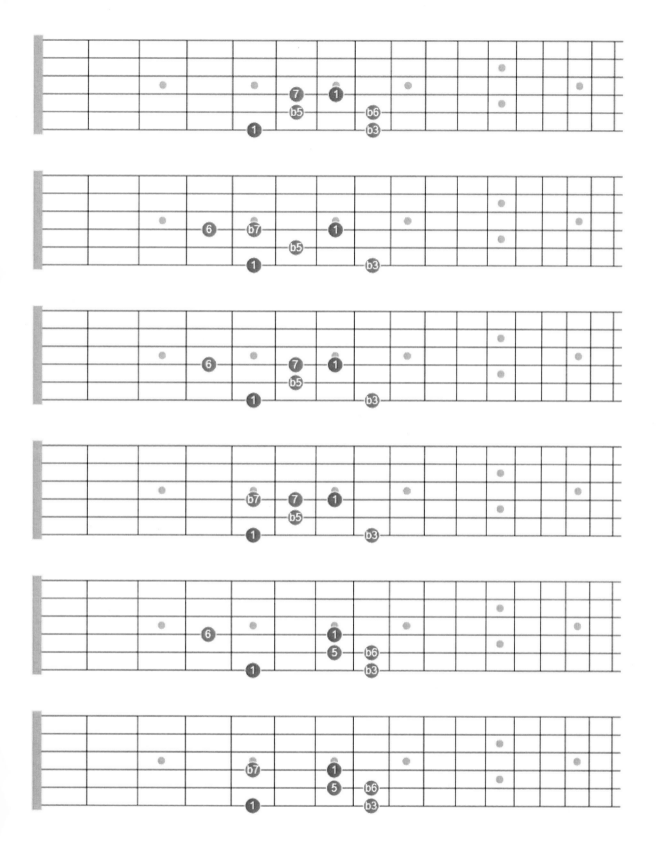

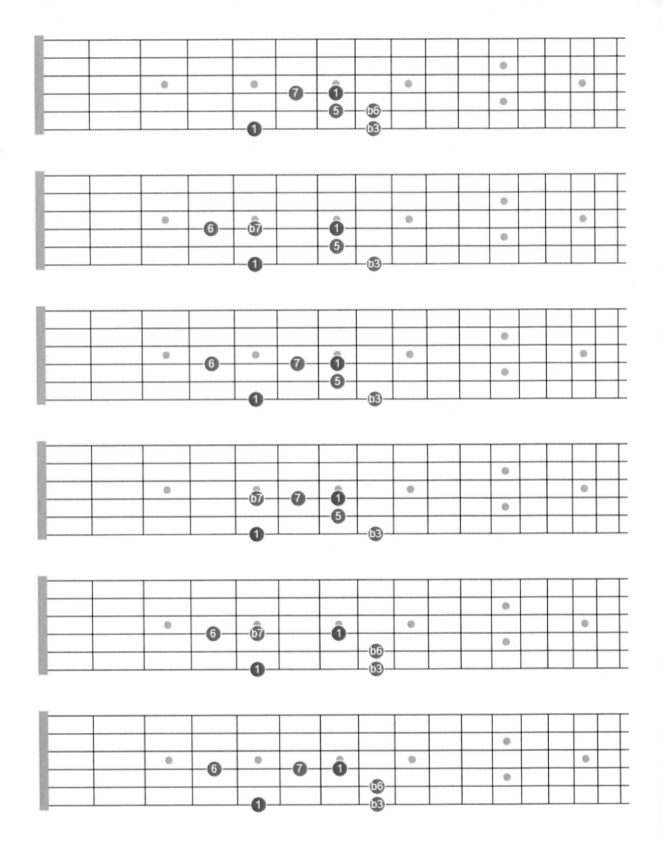

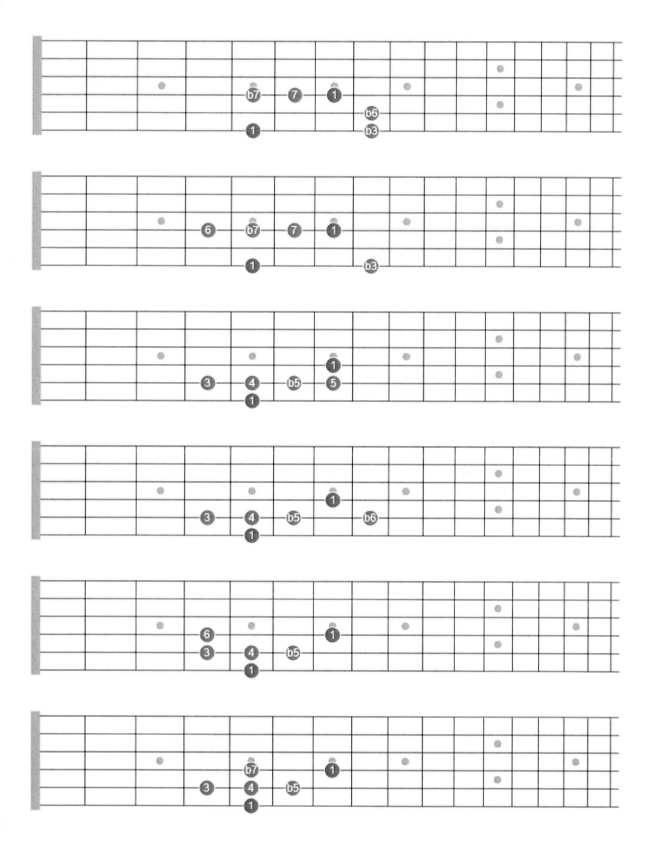

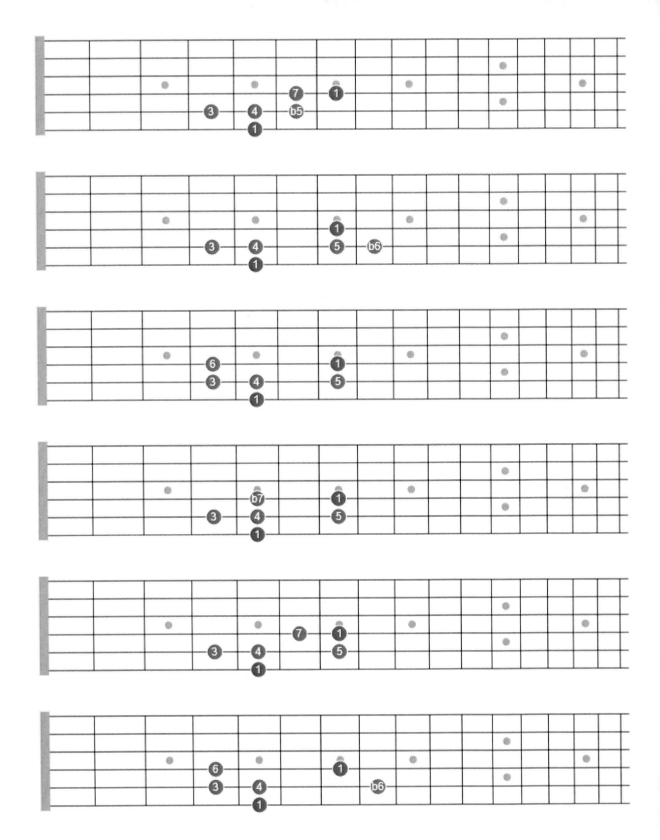

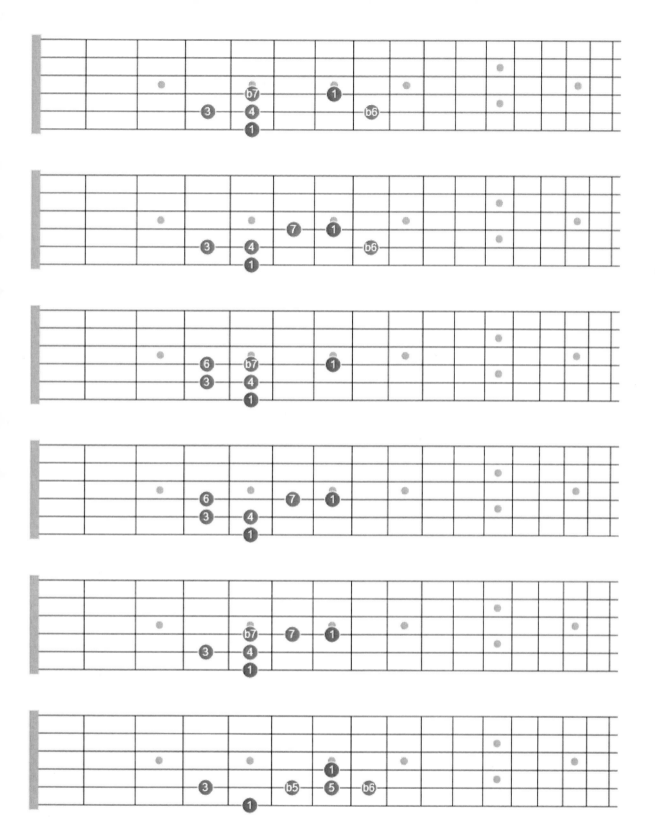

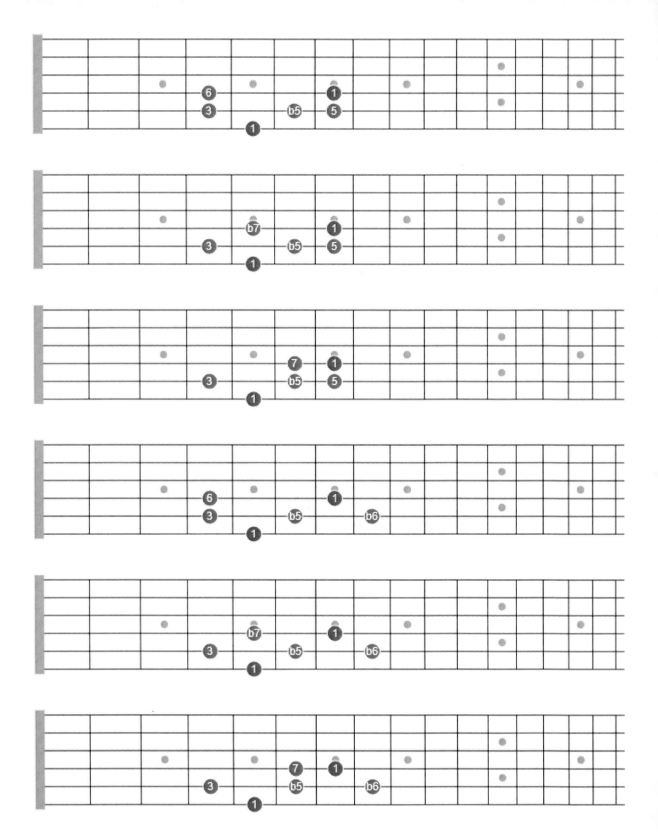

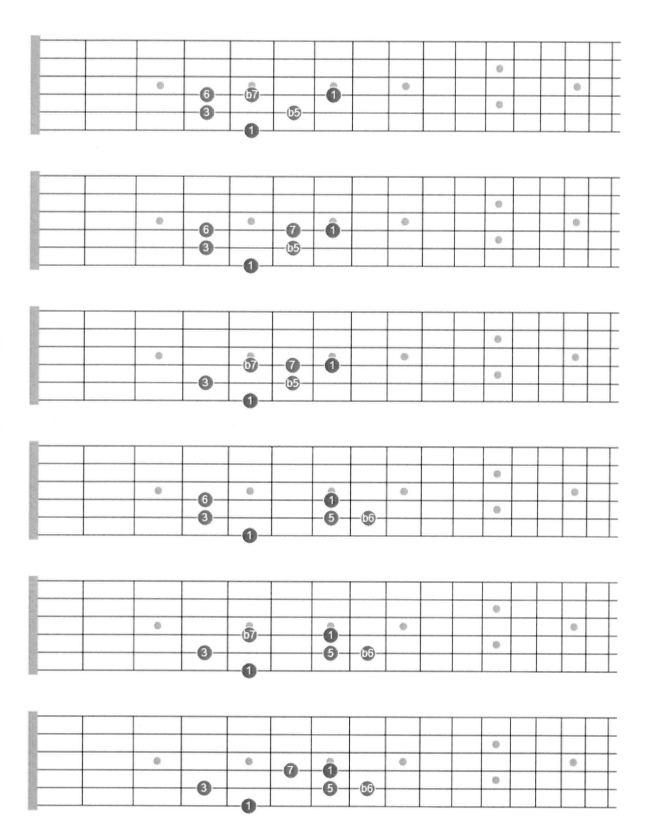

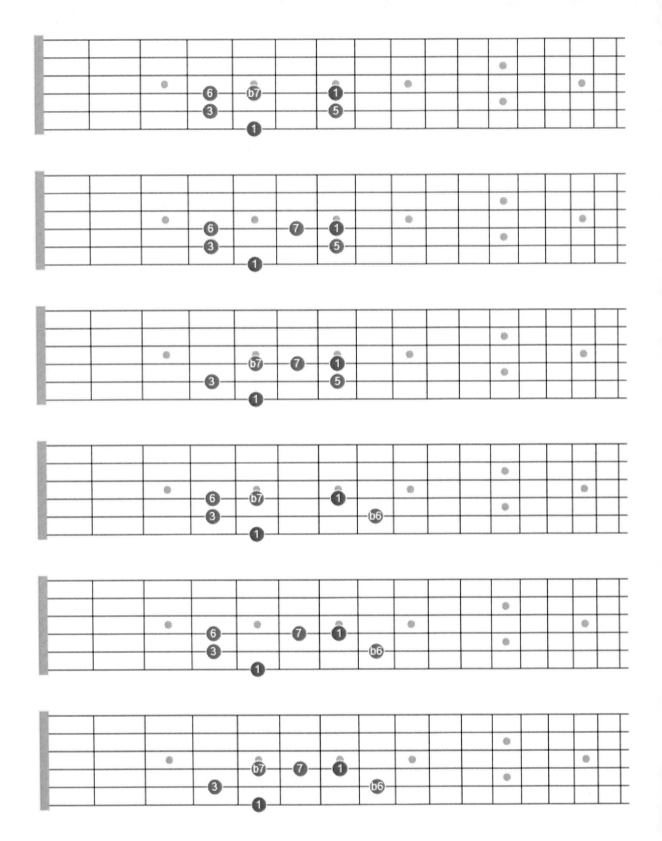

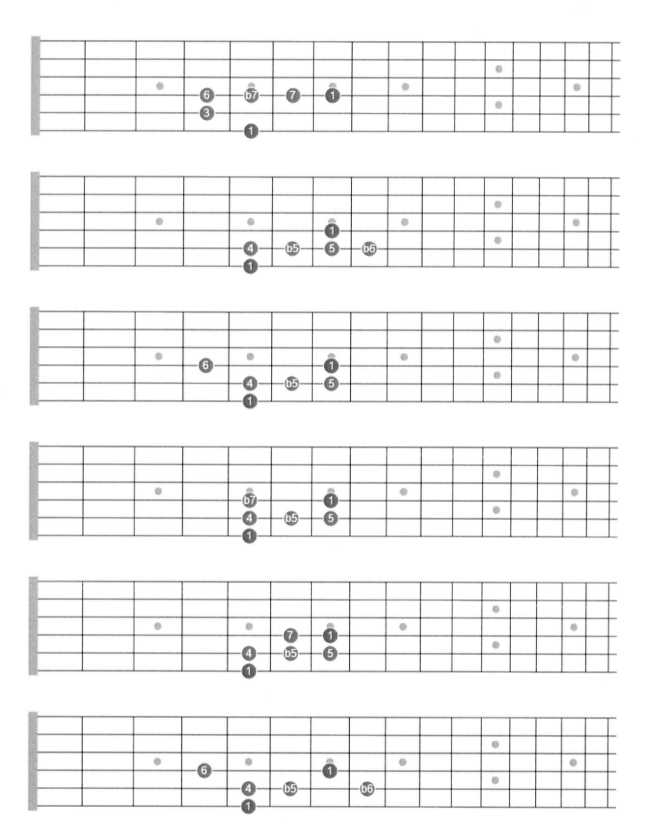

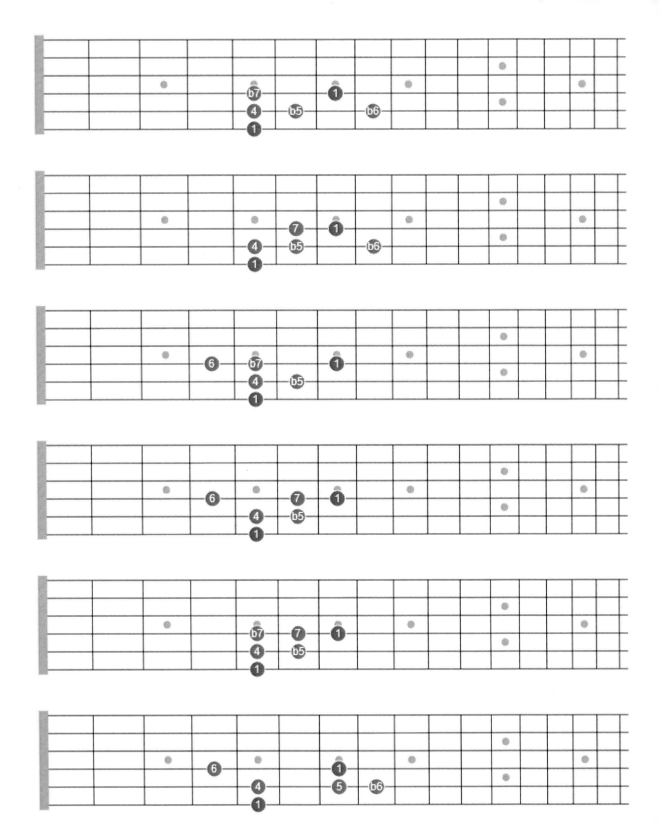

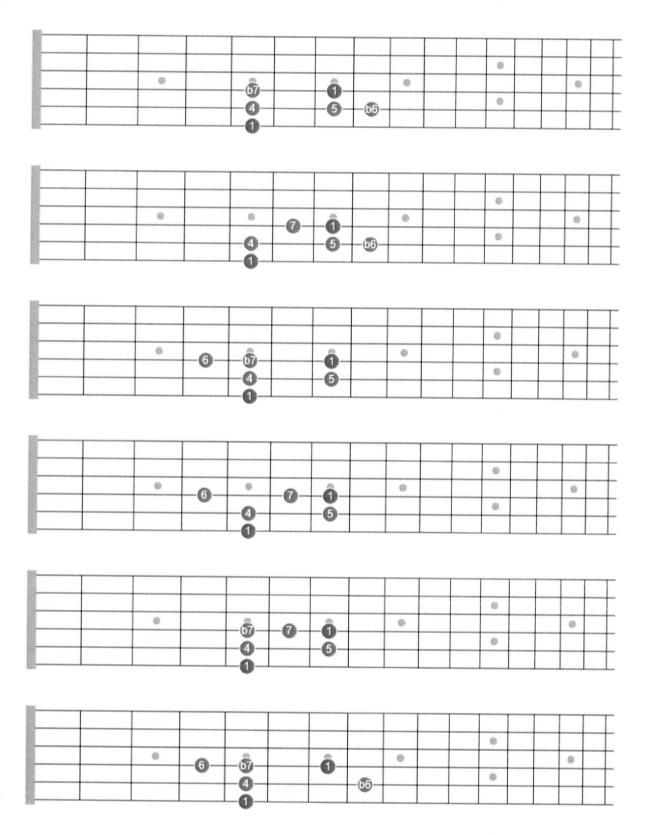

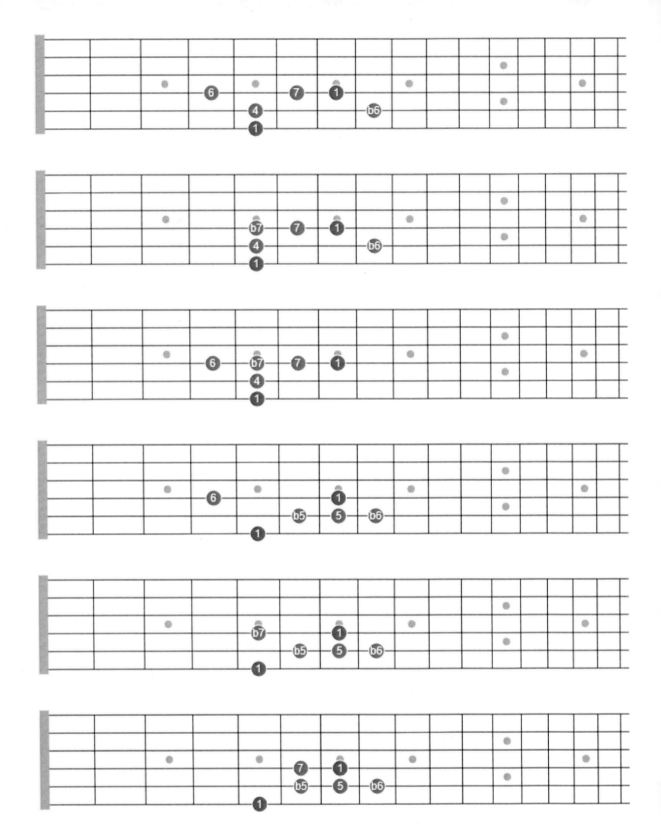

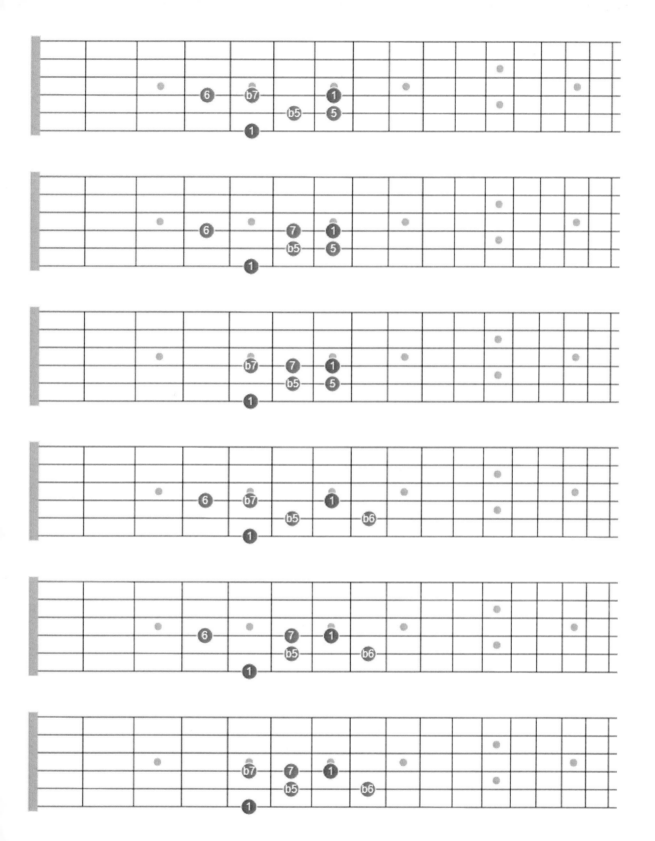

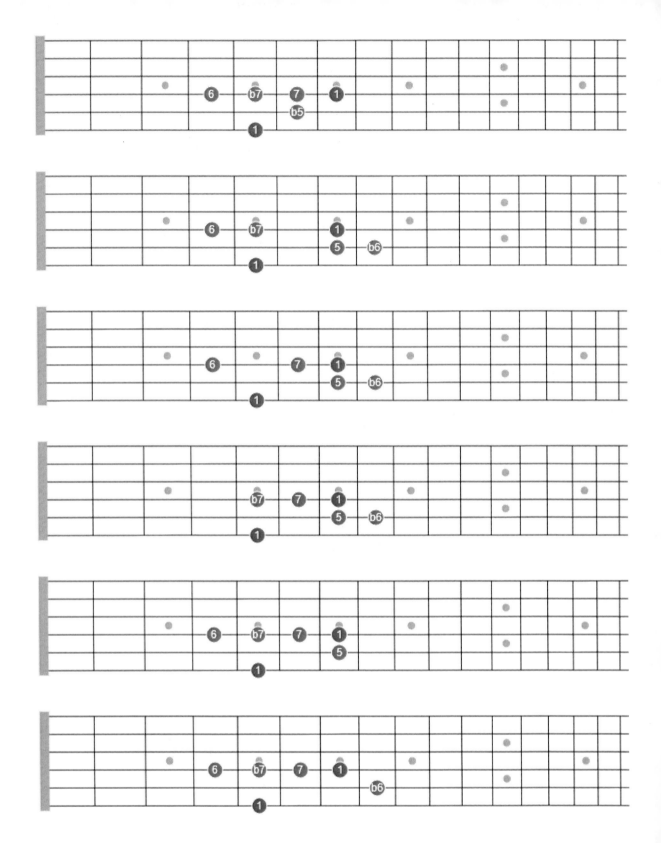

Made in United States
North Haven, CT
01 June 2022

19729286R00033